KV-190-395

Contents

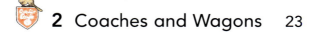

CAVAN COUNTY
LIBRARY

Smoke from the coal fire comes out through the smoke-stack.

Steam is made in the boiler. Water to make the steam is heated over a coal fire.

This is George Stephenson's *Invicta* steam locomotive. It is very like his famous *Rocket*.

1

Locomotives

The first railways were built in Europe nearly 500 years ago. The tracks were wooden. Horses pulled the wagons. They carried rocks and dirt out of mines.

About 200 years ago the first steam-powered locomotive was built in England. The best-known steam engine was the *Rocket*. George Stephenson built it in 1829. The *Rocket* could go as fast as 47 kilometres per hour!

Steam locomotives were used for over 100 years. Some are still in use today.

Wild West Locomotive

This American locomotive was built in 1857. By this time steam engines looked very different from the *Rocket*. American locos used wood fires to boil water for steam. Spark arresters on the smoke-stacks kept sparks from starting forest fires.

driver's cabin

boiler

The firebox is underneath the boiler.

driving wheels

Steam locos are named for the number of wheels they have, starting from the front. This is a 4-4-0 loco. It has 4 front bogie wheels, 4 big driving wheels and no rear bogies.

Locos like this one brought people to live in America's Wild West. They were used until about 1920.

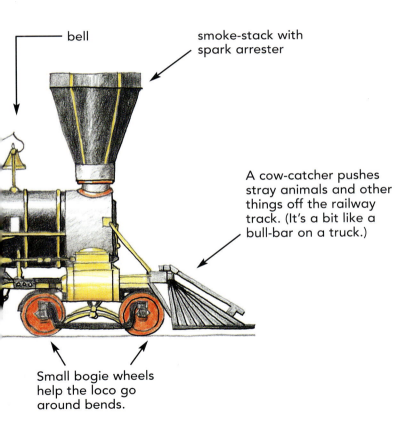

bell

smoke-stack with spark arrester

A cow-catcher pushes stray animals and other things off the railway track. (It's a bit like a bull-bar on a truck.)

Small bogie wheels help the loco go around bends.

German Heavyweight

This big steam locomotive was built in Germany around 1920. It pulled large trains between cities. Hundreds of these locos were used all over the world.

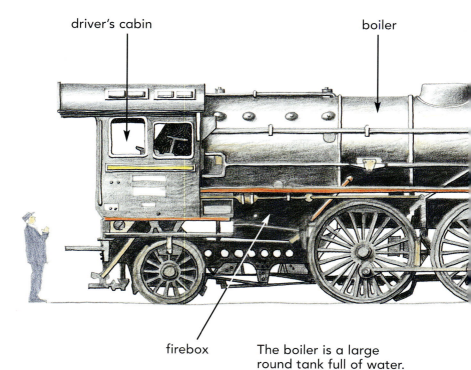

driver's cabin

boiler

firebox

The boiler is a large round tank full of water. Thin pipes inside the boiler carry hot air from the firebox. The hot air makes the water boil.

Steam from the boiler is piped into pistons. The steam expands (takes up more space), pushing long steel rods connected to the big driving wheels. This makes the wheels go round.

steam goes in here

rod

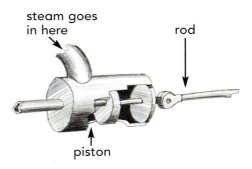

piston

Smoke from the fire comes out of the smoke-stack.

This is a 4-6-2 locomotive. It has 4 front bogies, 6 driving wheels and 2 rear bogies.

piston

American Super-heavyweight

This is Big Boy, the biggest steam engine ever made. It weighs 600 tonnes. A worker in the factory where the locos were built wrote "Big Boy" on one of them in chalk. The name has stuck.

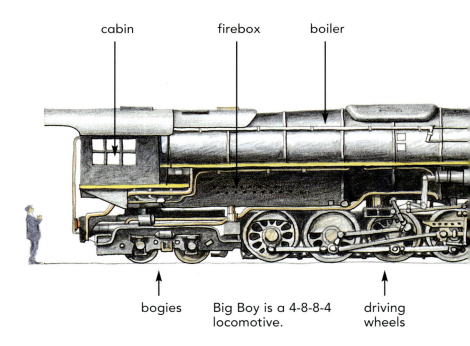

cabin   firebox   boiler

bogies   Big Boy is a 4-8-8-4 locomotive.   driving wheels

Twenty-five of these locos were made in the United States in 1941. They were used to pull heavy loads in hilly country.

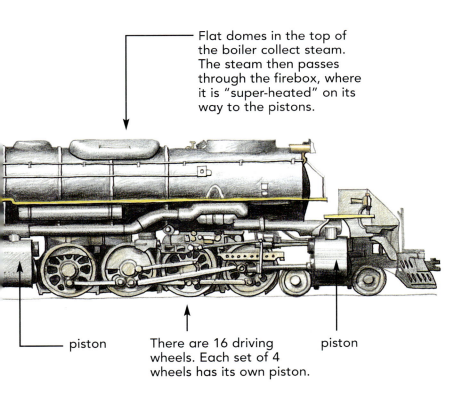

Flat domes in the top of the boiler collect steam. The steam then passes through the firebox, where it is "super-heated" on its way to the pistons.

piston

There are 16 driving wheels. Each set of 4 wheels has its own piston.

piston

Streamlined Train

By about 1930 rich people began to travel by aeroplane rather than by train. Plane travel was fast. Railway companies knew they had to build faster locomotives.

Air slows down anything that moves through it. If trains had clean, smooth lines, air would flow around them more easily. A new streamlined shape would make them go faster.

The trains didn't just need to *be* fast. They also had to *look* fast. Some of the bits on the front of this American steam engine are mostly for looks!

A special wagon called a tender carries water and fuel. It is hooked up right behind the steam engine.

The Crocodile

There are many mountains in Switzerland. Trains here need powerful locomotives to climb steep slopes. Steam engines can't go uphill easily. They also have problems with long mountain tunnels. All the smoke and steam has nowhere to go.

The Swiss Federal Railways built these locomotives in the 1920s. They were named "crocodiles" because they are long and low.

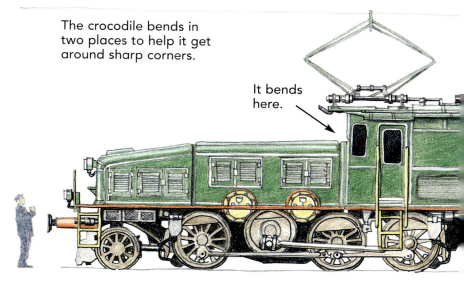

The crocodile bends in two places to help it get around sharp corners.

It bends here.

Crocodiles get their power from electrical wires above the railway track. Electricity is brought from the wire to the engine by a pantograph.

A crocodile has two locomotives, back to back. It can go in either direction without turning around.

A pantograph has springs in it. It can go up or down to adapt to the height of the overhead wire.

electrical wire

It bends here.

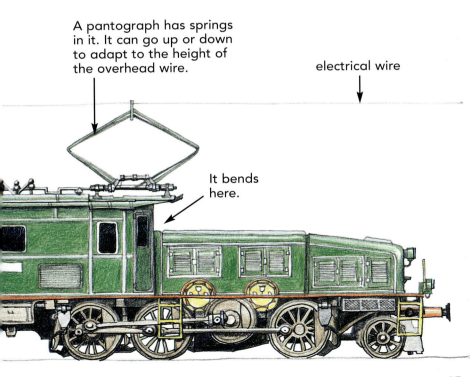

Diesel-electric Train

In the 1930s a very different kind of locomotive was built – the diesel-electric. It cost more to make than a steam engine, but it was faster. It was also cheaper to run.

The oil tender behind the second loco carries diesel fuel.

Two locomotives are working together here. The streamlined loco at the front has a driver's cabin and a headlight. The second loco has no driver. It is connected to the controls of the first one.

The diesel engine runs on diesel oil. The engine makes electricity. This powers the motors that turn the wheels. The number of motors depends on the size of the loco and what it has to do.

Today most railway engines are diesel-electric.

Diesel-electric Shunting Engine

This diesel-electric shunting engine works in a railway yard. It pushes and pulls empty wagons to make up trains.

Somebody has stuck this sign here as a joke. An express train is a fast long-distance train that doesn't stop anywhere along the way. A shunting engine moves slowly. It is always stopping and starting.

The driver looks out through this window.

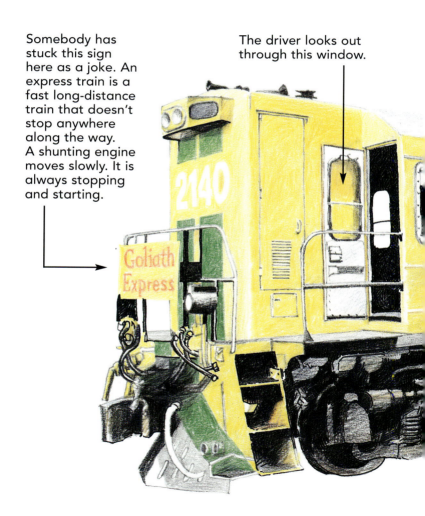

It also helps to load freight trains by pushing them slowly through freight-loading equipment.

High Speed Train

From about 1950 onwards, railway lines started to close down. It was faster and easier to travel by car or plane. Trains were just too slow. They also cost a lot to build and run.

Japan's Bullet Train (the Shinkansen R-500) has an electric motor on every axle of every carriage.

Japan is a country that has lots of earthquakes. If there is even a small earthquake, the Bullet Train stops automatically.

Then, in around 1980, people in Japan and Europe started working on new "very fast trains".

These sleek, modern electric trains run on a normal railway with concrete sleepers. They can travel at up to 500 kilometres an hour.

Now, in some places, trains go from city to city almost as quickly as planes do.

Experimental Trains

Better, faster trains are always being invented. Some of the latest have wheels with rubber tyres. Some just float along, held up by powerful magnets. One new kind of train in France doesn't even need a driver.

This train leans over when it goes around a corner. (You do the same thing when you're riding a bike.)

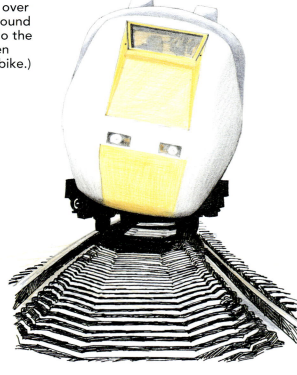

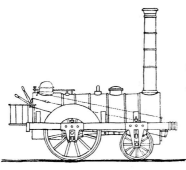

2

Coaches and Wagons

The wagons or coaches pulled by the locomotive make up the "train". Wagons carry freight (goods or cargo). Coaches, or carriages, carry people.

Many wagons are built to carry just one sort of cargo, like wheat or petrol. A train is the best way to transport bulk goods over long distances.

Most passenger trains are local or commuter trains. They carry people only for short distances. Long-distance passenger trains are fun to ride on. If you travel at night, you might have your own bed in a sleeping coach!

Box Car

Box cars have sides, doors and a roof. They carry anything that could be damaged by weather. Their cargo might be parcels, furniture, books or newspapers.

This is a ventilated box car. It can carry fresh fruit and vegetables, or live animals. Slots in the sides let air flow in and out.

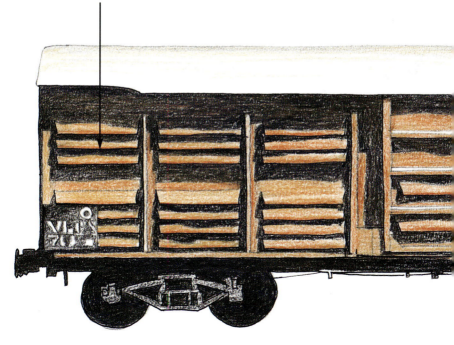

Box cars are not used much today. They take too long to load and unload. It is cheaper and easier to carry goods in bulk, or in containers (see pages 28-29).

Open Wagon

Open wagons carry goods that can't be spoiled by rain. Cranes make loading and unloading easy.

This wagon was not built to carry any special sort of cargo. It could be used for timber, large machinery, cars, minerals, gravel, pipes or steel.

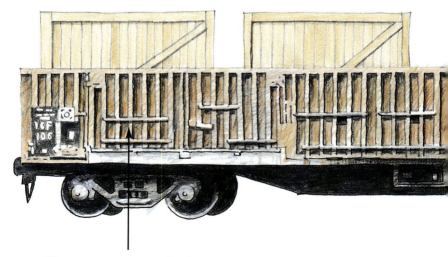

There are gates on both sides of the wagon.

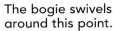

The bogie swivels around this point.

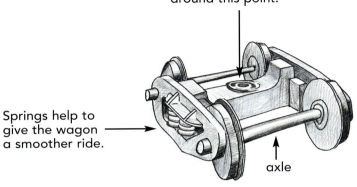

Springs help to give the wagon a smoother ride.

axle

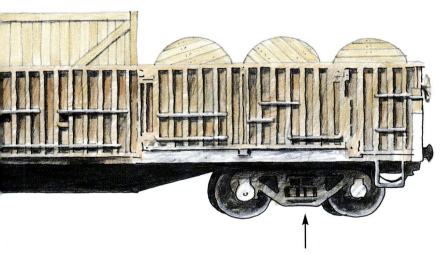

Most goods wagons sit on two 4-wheel bogies or "trucks". The bogies swivel when the train goes around a curve.

Flat Car

Flat cars are used to move cars and trucks, timber, and even blocks of stone.

The wagon shown here carries containers. These are big steel and aluminium boxes that can be filled with most kinds of cargo.

The containers on this flat car belong to a large shipping company.

It takes a long time to unload lots
of small boxes from a train and then
re-load them onto a truck or ship.
Containers are unloaded very quickly,
using a crane.

Some containers are kept cool inside,
like a fridge. They carry fresh foods
like meat and vegetables.

Loading and
Unloading Containers

Containers are made in only two sizes. All over the world trains, trucks, ships and aircraft are built to carry these two sizes of boxes.

Containers are loaded and unloaded at container terminals. Here big cranes move the containers from one sort of transport to another.

A crane hooks into the top four corners of the container. It lifts it off the truck and puts it down on the flat car.

31

Mineral Wagon

This open wagon can load about
60 tonnes of minerals, sand or gravel.
This is twice as much as a large truck
can carry. Some larger 16-wheeled
wagons carry as much as 125 tonnes.

There is a hatch or "gate" in the floor of this wagon. When the gate opens, the load pours out into trucks or onto a conveyor belt below.

This round handle opens the "gate".

Bulk Grain Carrier

Loads like wheat and cement will spoil if they get wet. They must be carried in enclosed wagons like this one.

This ladder leads to a walkway along the top of the wagon. Workers climb up here to open the lids.

walkway

lids

Some grain carriers don't have to stop to unload. They slow down to about 3 kilometres per hour. Chutes in the bottom of the wagon open to dump the grain in long bins below the rails.

Grain silos stand beside the railway line. Special chutes in the silos pour grain into these openings.

These chutes open to unload the grain into trucks or storage bins.

Bulk Liquid Tanker

Many liquids are carried by train in huge tankers. Petrol, oil, paint, chemicals, milk and fruit juices are some that are carried this way. Some towns in outback Australia even have their water brought to them by train.

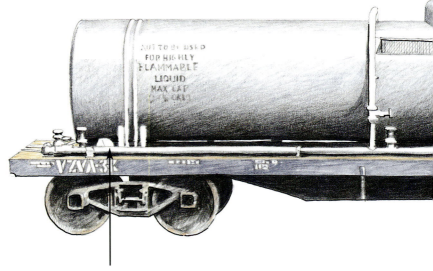

Liquid is pumped in and out through these pipes.

Each tanker can only be used to carry one liquid. It would not be a good idea to carry milk in a tanker which has held a poisonous chemical!

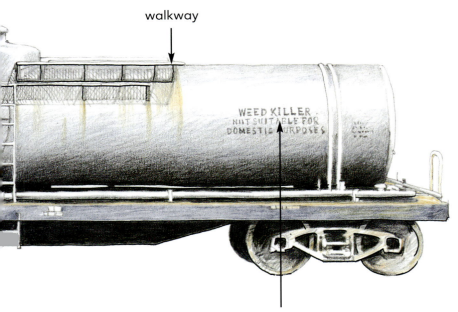

walkway

WEED KILLER
NOT SUITABLE FOR
DOMESTIC PURPOSES

Workers need to get inside the tank to clean it. A ladder and walkways allow them to reach the opening in the top of the tank.

Signs printed on the tank say what it is used for.

Passenger Coaches

Some passenger coaches can be very uncomfortable. The commuter trains that take people to and from work are often crowded. They are built to hold as many passengers as possible. Many people have to stand up.

Special windows called "observation domes" let people look up at the tops of the mountains.

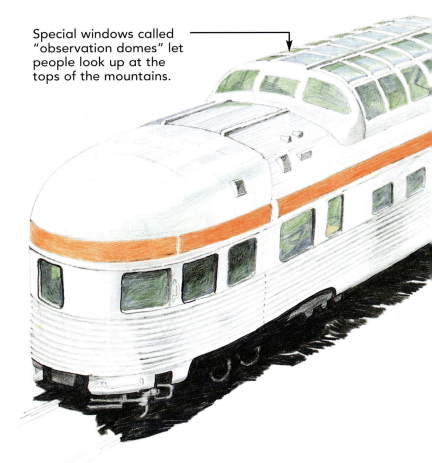

This Canadian Pacific Railways train is built for long-distance travel. It takes passengers across the Rocky Mountains in the west of Canada.

The coaches of long-distance trains are very different. They have sleeping coaches, restaurant coaches and bars. People can relax in comfort and enjoy their journey.

Brake Van

Before wagons had their own brakes, a brake van was hitched to the end of the train. If a wagon broke loose, the back of the train could roll away, out of control. The guard used the brakes in the brake van to stop this part of the train.

Today, brakes on all wagons are operated by the train driver. In an emergency they work by themselves.

The brake van (sometimes known as a guard's van or caboose) was also used to carry luggage and parcels.

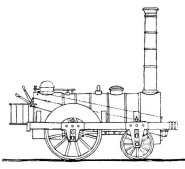

3

Special Purpose Trains

Most trains are built to do only one thing. Some transport minerals from a mine to a port. Others take people from one city to another, or carry timber from a mill to a big city.

The locomotive and the carriages are specially made to go together. They can't work in any other way. They can't be used with other carriages or other locomotives.

Fast Inter-city Passenger Train

The *Eurostar* runs in England, France, Belgium and Germany. It is an electric train. It can run on the different power supplies in each of the four countries.

The locomotive and carriages are made to go together.

The height of railway platforms is different for each country, too. When the *Eurostar* arrives at a station, the steps from each carriage door fold down to exactly the right height for the platform.

Commuter Train

This suburban commuter train carries people from one part of a big city to another. Most of its passengers are on their way to or from work. Like most suburban trains, it runs on electricity.

Some commuter trains travel underground. They go through special tunnels deep below the city. Even the stations are underground. Passengers go down long escalators to get to them.

The notice in the window tells us that this train is a Race Special. It is taking people to the horse races.

Pantographs (see page 15) carry electricity from overhead power lines to the train's electric motors.

RACE SPECIAL

Monorail

A monorail is a train that runs on just one rail, not two. The rail is usually built high above the ground, on pillars. Monorails are used in city areas where there is no room to build a normal railway.

This monorail in Tokyo, Japan, goes from the airport to the city centre. It runs on a heavy concrete beam. Electric power for the train comes from a wire that runs along the side of the beam.

A monorail always runs on the same line. It can't turn off from one line on to another.

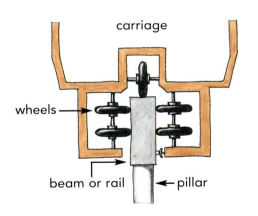

carriage

wheels

beam or rail

pillar

At each end of the carriage there are two sets of five wheels. One wheel runs on top of the beam to carry the weight of the carriage. The other four run along the sides of the beam to stop the carriage from tipping over. All the wheels have rubber tyres.

Mineral Train

This railway line was built just to carry iron ore. It runs from Mount Tom Price, where the ore is mined, to the port of Dampier in Western Australia.

Long, heavy trains run from the mine to the port and back again, all day, every day.

Two big diesel-electric locomotives are needed to pull this heavy load.

At Dampier the trains drop the ore on
conveyor belts. The belts load the
ore straight onto ships.

Sugar-cane Train

In North Queensland many sugar-cane farms have their very own railway lines. At harvest time, little engines tow long lines of wagons through the cane fields. They carry the cut cane to crushing plants near by.

The smoke-stack has a spark arrester. It looks a bit like the one on the old Wild West loco (pages 6-7).

Many sugar-cane locomotives, like this one, used to run on steam. Most now have diesel engines.

Brightly coloured stripes make the engine easy to see. This helps to prevent accidents.

Cog Railway

Most trains are too heavy to go up steep slopes, so railway builders try to avoid hills. Sometimes the railway line goes around them. Sometimes it tunnels right through the middle of them.

Some special trains *do* go uphill. The cog or "rack" railway shown here has a big cog wheel. The wheel pushes the engine up the hill. It "climbs" a toothed rail fixed between two normal rails.

Cable railways are also built to climb hills. The train is pulled uphill by a long steel cable.

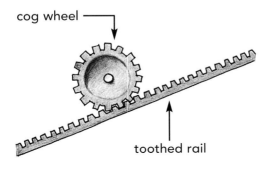

cog wheel

toothed rail

coal tender

The boiler is behind the cabin.

cabin

9

The locomotive slopes downwards from one end to the other. This is because steam engine boilers don't work very well on a hill. When the cog railway train is going up a steep hill, the sloping locomotive becomes nearly level.

Snow Plough

Unlike planes and cars, trains can keep going in bad weather. Even snowstorms don't stop them!

The whistle sounds when the driver lets a little steam out of the boiler.

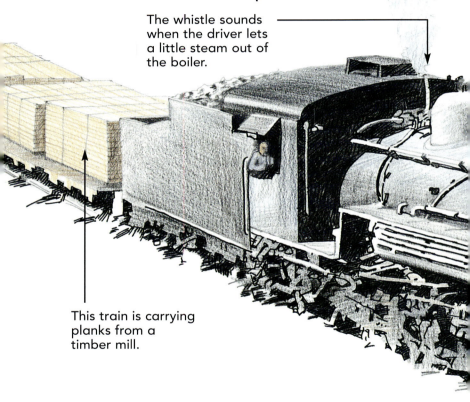

This train is carrying planks from a timber mill.

When lots of trains use the same railway, a special snow plough train goes along the line first. It clears away the snow for all the other trains.

When snow piles up on roads, cars must wait while snow-blowers clear the way for them. A locomotive with a snow plough fitted to the front can clear its own way.

The snow plough can be taken off when it is not needed.

Breakdown Train

Railway transport is very safe. Trains travel on rails, so they can't run into trees. They can't try to overtake each other, either. But sometimes trains *do* have accidents. Often a breakdown train is called in to help.

Workers wear jackets with bright yellow squares so they can be seen easily by the crane drivers.

This worker is helping to pass a heavy chain under the loco so the crane can lift it.

This picture shows a breakdown train at the scene of an accident. A train has come off the railway track. The big crane on the breakdown train will lift it back onto the rails.

Track-laying Train

New railways are still being built all over the world, and old lines have to be mended. Steel rails last for only 15 to 20 years. Wooden sleepers need to be replaced.

The first railway tracks were built by lots of people using simple tools like hammers and shovels. These days, tracks are laid by special trains like the one shown here.

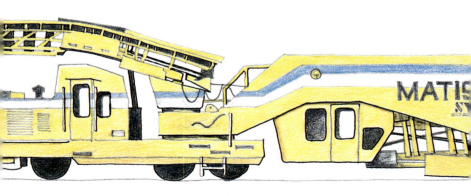

Steel train wheels have flanges to keep them on the rails.

Rails are fixed to wooden or concrete sleepers or cross-ties.

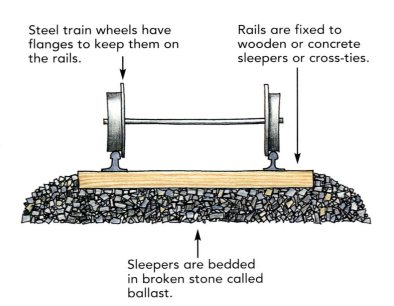

Sleepers are bedded in broken stone called ballast.

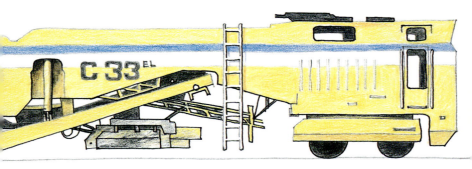

C 33 EL

Signals

Train drivers must know if the line ahead is clear of other trains. In the early days, policemen gave signals to tell the driver when it was safe to drive on. Later, mechanical signals told the driver what to do. Still later a system of lights (like traffic lights) was used.

Today, signals are given by tiny electronic "transponders" fixed to the rails. They tell the driver and the train's computerised control system which trains have passed over them, and when. If something is not right, the transponders can stop the train.

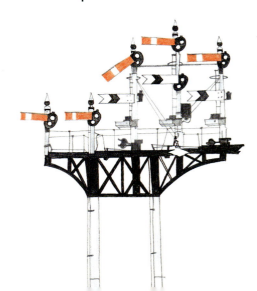

Each of these mechanical railway signals gives a message in code to the train driver.

Railway Liveries

Every train is painted with its own design and colours. This is known as its *livery*.

All railway companies have their own livery. Each also has its own company badge or logo. Here are some of them, past and present:

Austrian State Railways

British Rail

Canadian Pacific Railways

Central Railroad of New Jersey (USA)

Danish State Railways

Mount Newman Railroad (Australia)

Atchison, Topeka and Santa Fe (USA)

Société Nationale des Chemins de Fer (France)

Glossary

axle ∗ The rod that goes through the centre of a wheel or wheels.

bogie ∗ A small frame with wheels that sits under the end of a locomotive or wagon. It swivels to allow the wagon or locomotive to go around bends.

bulk ∗ Loose cargo (like sand, wheat or water).

cargo ∗ A load.

chute ∗ A slide or sloping channel. Things pour down a chute from one container to a lower container.

cog wheel ∗ A wheel with cogs or "teeth" that lock into the teeth on another cog wheel or a rail.

commuter ∗ A person who travels to and from work in a train, bus or car.

conveyor belt ∗ An endless moving belt or loop, usually made of flat rubber. As it moves, it carries cargo from one place to another.

diesel engine ∗ An engine that works like a petrol-driven engine, but uses thicker "diesel" fuel.

electronic ∗ Worked by the movement of millions of tiny electrons. Electrons carry electricity.

enclosed ∗ Shut in on all sides, and at the top and bottom.

flange ∗ A jutting edge on the rim of a wheel.

locomotive ∗ An engine used for pulling trains.

mechanical ∗ Worked by a machine (instead of a person).

freight ✳ Goods carried from one place to another. A *freight train* is a train that carries goods rather than passengers.

ore ✳ Rock that contains minerals or metals such as iron.

piston ✳ A disc or round plate which slides up and down inside a tube or cylinder.

snow-blower ✳ A giant vacuum-cleaner used to suck snow off a road and blow it out to one side, so that cars can use the road.

swivel ✳ Rotate or spin around something fixed, like a wheel around an axle or like a spinning top.

terminal ✳ A place where passengers get on or off buses, trains or aircraft, or where cargo is loaded or unloaded.

ventilated ✳ Provided with holes so air can get in and out.

Index